The
World's Best
Cricket Jokes

The World's Best Cricket Jokes

Ernest Forbes

Illustrated by Tony Blundell

HarperCollins*Publishers*

HarperCollins*Publishers*
77–85 Fulham Palace Road,
Hammersmith, London W6 8JB

This paperback edition 1994
1 3 5 7 9 8 6 4 2

Previously published in paperback by Fontana 1993

First published in Great Britain by
Angus & Robertson Publishers (UK) 1988
Reprinted once

Text copyright © Ernest Forbes 1988
Illustrations copyright © Angus & Robertson 1988

The Author asserts the moral right to
be identified as the author of this work

ISBN 0 00 638080 8

Set in Goudy

Printed in Great Britain by
HarperCollinsManufacturing Glasgow

He had just received the award for the best batting average of the season.

In his speech of thanks he said it was mainly due to his wife that he received the award. 'At the beginning of the season my wife and I agreed that whenever we had an argument the one who was wrong would pay a little forfeit. Mine was to have an extra two hours at the nets and my wife was to work for two hours in the garden. That is why I have the best betting average and the worst garden in the country.'

Cricketer: 'Doctor, I'm having a terrible time. I'm not getting any runs, my ground fielding is dreadful and I can't hold my catches. What should I do?'

Doctor: 'Try a different sport.'

Cricketer: 'I can't. I'm captain of England!'

'Boy, that bowler is good,' said the American, 'he hits that bat right in the middle every goddam time.'

In a paternity case against a well-known Test cricketer the plaintiff was asked on what grounds the case was based. The reply was quick and to the point, 'Lords, The Gabba, Faizabad and Karachi.'

The two Royal Navy chaplins sat in the members' stand watching a hard-fought match between an Army XI and a Royal Navy XI. One chaplin nudged his colleague, 'You know, cricket really is a wonderful game, the perfect expression of sportsmanship and fair play. Here we are watching a battle between two great services and the important thing is not who wins but how the game is played.' He paused, 'Providing, of course, we beat those Army bastards!'

'I've never umpired a cricket match before. Do I have to run after the ball?'
'No, after the match.'

It is rumoured that a Test cricketer once remarked, 'When you bat with Kapel Dev you don't call – you pray!'

She: 'Oh darling, I'm looking forward to our wedding and all your cricketing friends making an arch for us by holding up their bats, just like they did for Mike.'

He: 'I don't think we'll have an arch, dear.'

She: 'Why not, darling?'

He: 'They held up their bats because he was a batsman.'

She: 'So?'

He: 'I'm a bowler!'

'I've been invited to join Essex, they want me to play for them very badly.'

'Well in that case you're just the man.'

It was the after-lunch session, and the next batsman in hadn't left the bar. When it was his turn to bat he confessed to the captain that he could see three of everything.

'Well,' said the captain, 'when you get out to the wicket just hit the middle ball.'

The batsman made his way to the middle and was bowled first ball.

'What happened?' asked the captain. 'Did you play the wrong ball?'

'No, the wrong bowler!'

The public school was at home to a cricket eleven from the coal mines.

A miner approached the school captain. 'Here, where are your bowlers?'

'Oh, we don't wear bowlers, we have caps.'

He was tall, good looking, charming and a first-class batsman and some surprise was shown when he refused to coach the ladies in the art of batsmanship. When he was asked why he refused he stroked his chin thoughtfully and replied, 'Well, if I were to coach them I would be telling them to keep their legs close together and that would go against my nature.'

In a London court a man was charged with attempted arson. In reply to the charge of trying to set fire to the new stand at Lords the man said he had a burning interest in cricket.

'You need glasses,' growled the dismissed batsman as he passed the man in the white coat.
'So do you, mate,' answered the man. 'I'm selling ice cream.'

During the match the wicket-keeper employed all the old tricks to try and distract the batsman, tapping his gloves, coughing, moving almost level in line with the stumps.

The moves must have upset the batsman for he was rapped on the pads three times but each time the appeal was turned down. The umpire turned to the wicket-keeper: 'I've been watching you the last few overs.'

'I thought so,' replied the wicket-keeper. 'I knew you weren't watching the game.'

Greek spectator to his brother: 'I don't know what you think of this cricket but it's all English to me.'

Last night at the annual cricket club dance the music was so bad that when someone sounded the fire alarm everyone got up to dance.

It was the annual match between the local team and a team of ladies. The men won the toss and elected to bat. The opening batsman was about to indicate two leg as a guard when he realised a lady was umpiring, so he didn't sign for a guard but began to make his mark.

The lady umpire watched him for a moment then shouted, 'Do you want two leg, or what?'

The batsman smiled and said, 'I'd rather have "what" but I supposed we'd better play cricket first.'

A young Irish cricketer on tour in Canada was delighted when he was given a room with running water as he had always wanted to meet a Red Indian.

The batsman kept looking at the members' stand. Before he played a ball he would look at the stand.

The wicket-keeper watched him with great interest, then remarked, 'Do you think you can hook it into the stand?'

'It's just that my mother-in-law is sitting in the stand.'

'Dammit man, you'll never hit her from here!'

*B*owler: 'I had three catches dropped today.'

Captain: 'Yes, but they were all dropped by spectators in the stand!'

*W*ife: 'Cricket! Cricket! Cricket! That's all you think about. If you mention cricket once again I'll die, that's what I'll do, just die!'

Husband (bowling an off spinner with an orange): 'Promises! Promises! Promises!'

The touring captain called the batsman to one side. 'Tomorrow's test is going to be tough. These West Indians bowl even faster in front of their home crowd. I want to talk to you because I need a batsman with great concentration, good eye, strong constitution and who can really stand up to fast bowling, so that's why I'm making you twelfth man.'

'How long were you in the first eleven?'
'Oh, about five feet eight inches.'

A famous Hollywood film actress was on her first visit to India and was very interested in going to Calcutta during a Test match. She got VIP treatment and enjoyed the lead-up to the first over, the captains tossing, the white-clad players taking the field and the arrival of the batsmen. The opening batsman scored a boundary off the sixth ball and the umpire called, 'Over'.

'Well,' said the actress rising, 'it really is a beautiful game, but it's so very short!'

The reason so many cricketers look weather-beaten is that rain stops play so often.

The bowler drank his beer slowly and thoughtfully. He had taken a lot of stick that afternoon and had ended with 0 for 112. His captain was sympathetic: 'One of those days. Don't worry, you'll be in better form next week.'

The bowler looked at him in surprise: 'Me in better form? I was in good form; the fielders are to blame, they let me down.'

'Dammit Clive, there wasn't one dropped catch!'

'I know that,' retorted the bowler, 'but I was bowling for run-outs!'

A streaker who ran onto the playing area at the Adelaide Oval during a Test match was caught by the short leg and led off.

First MCC Member: 'My wife's in bed with shingles.'

Second MCC Member: 'Nice chap, Shingles. Used to open the innings with him at Oxford.'

The batsman was out first ball. On the long walk back to the pavilion he had to pass the incoming batsman.

'Hard luck,' sneered the new batsman.

'Yes. It's a shame that I had to be in the middle of a hat trick!'

When Bill 'Tiger' O'Reilly, the great Australian fast bowler, was in England on tour he attended a party given by a Peer of the Realm.

The hostess indicated to the bowler and asked Lindsay Hassett who he was.

'That's Tiger,' answered Lindsay Hassett.

'Oh, really?' exclaimed the hostess.

'No, ma'am, O'Reilly.'

'He must be an Irish cricketer.'
'Why?'
'He has his pads strapped onto his wellies.'

Then there was the girl who wanted a date with the fast bowler because she heard he had a good line and length.

Announcement *at a village cricket match:* 'For the benefit of the players here are the names of the spectators.'

'I can't understand it,' said the dismissed batsman. 'The ball hit my head and first slip caught it and the umpire gave me out.'
'I know,' said his friend. 'Sometimes they go by the sound.'

'If W. G. Grace were here today I wonder
how he would play in this limited-over
cricket?'

'Not very well I should think. He'd be over
one hundred and fifty years old!'

'Can I have your autograph, mister?' the boy
asked the cricketer.

The cricketer tried to brush him off. 'I really
don't play cricket,' he said.

'I know that,' replied the boy, 'but I'd like to
have it anyway!'

The bowler had just gone in to bat when the
telephone rang in the pavilion. A player
answered it to be told it was the bowler's wife and
she wanted to speak to her husband.

'I'm sorry, but he's just gone in to bat.'

'Oh, that's all right,' replied the wife. 'I'll hold
on!'

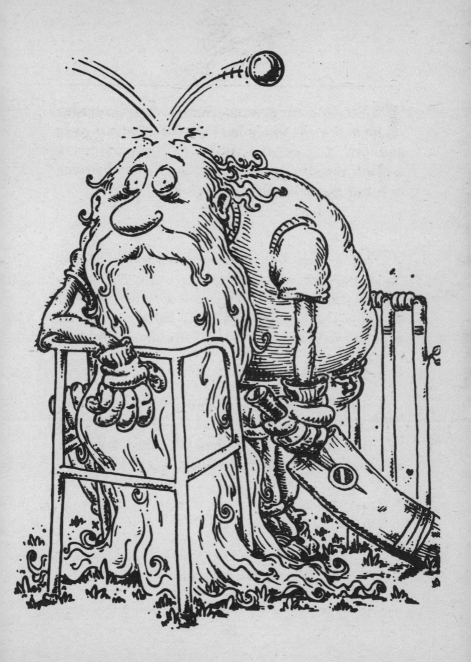

During the second day of the Test match at Lords the Queen paid a visit to the ground and play was stopped while the teams were pre sented to her.

It was a case of reign stopped play.

Owing to a clerical error, castor oil instead of salad oil was delivered to the Melbourne Cricket Club where the third Test match is being played. The Australians are batting and are expected to make a lot of runs this afternoon.

A word of advice was given by the senior professional to the new cricket captain. 'If I can be of any help just ask. You know two heads are better than one – especially if they are on a coin.'

The fast bowler had been bowling well without any luck and the captain suggested he take a break and one of the spinners come on.

The huge frame of the fast bowler heaved as he asked, 'Who had you in mind, skipper?'

'Phillips,' answered the captain.

'Phillips!' exclaimed the fast bowler. 'Why, he couldn't bowl a hoop down a hill!'

'Can he bowl a Chinaman?'

'He couldn't bowl a delph dog.'

Captain (to dismissed batsman): 'What happened?'

Batsman: 'The ball came back very quickly.'

Captain: 'And so did you.'

The Devil proposed a cricket match between Heaven and Hell. Saint Peter smiled, 'It wouldn't be fair for we have all the cricketers.'

'Ah,' pointed out the Devil. 'We have all the umpires.'

'Cricket, cricket, cricket,' the wife nagged. 'That's all you ever think of. Why, I bet you don't even remember the day we were married!'

'Of course I do,' replied the husband. 'It was the day Denis Compton scored 107 against Yorkshire.'

At the Lords Taverners' Annual Ball held at Lords Cricket Ground last night Raquel Welch and Elizabeth Taylor were refused admittance as the President had ruled out bouncers.

The batsman stormed into the pavilion and growled, 'That umpire who gave me out lbw should be carrying a white stick.'

'Did you get his name?'

'No, but I'd know his laugh anywhere!'

It is said of Imran Khan that he is the only player to call his partner for a run and wish him good luck at the same time.

W. G. Grace stroked his beard as he asked, 'Tell me, Murdoch, how many great players have you played against?'

'One less than you think,' replied the Australian captain.

It was a return match and the batsman was out first ball.

'Not like last week,' grinned the happy bowler.

'Not likely,' said the batsman. 'Last week I carried my bat for 112, and when I went in all the beer was gone!'

The office boy had asked for the afternoon off to attend his uncle's funeral. Instead, he went to a cricket match where the score was 220 for 0. Suddenly he felt a tap on his shoulder and there was his boss.

'So this is your uncle's funeral?' asked the boss.

'Looks like it,' replied the boy, 'he's the bowler!'

What is higher than an Australian cricket captain?

His cap.

The bowler got the batsman to snick a fast rising ball and the first slip took it cleanly. The umpire said, 'Not out.' The next ball was also caught, this time by the wicket-keeper. 'Not out,' said the umpire. The bowler's next delivery was unplayable and completely shattered the wicket. The bowler looked at the umpire and remarked quietly, 'That must have been quite close!'

The visitor was delighted as he looked around the room. It was full of cricket paraphernalia. A couple of bats, caps, a box with a dent, trophies and scores of photographs and newspaper cuttings.

As he examined some of the trophies, he noticed a small tarnished and uncared-for looking urn on the top shelf of a bookcase.

'What's this?' he asked, lifting the urn.

'The ashes,' grunted the host.

'The ashes!' exclaimed the visitor. 'Why are they not in pride of place?'

'Don't see why they should be,' replied his host, 'the wife never cared for cricket!'

The captain was giving the young batsman some advice. 'Now, when you go in, watch that slow left hand bowler very carefully. Keep your eye on the ball from when it leaves the bowler's hand and watch it all the way.'

'Never mind the bowler,' growled the old hand. 'Watch the umpire; that's his father!'

It was his first match for the second eleven and he was very nervous. He was lucky to have survived the first over. As the square leg umpire moved in, the batsman stammered, 'I suppose you've seen worse players.'

The umpire fiddled with a pencil he had in his hand.

The batsman spoke again, 'I expect you've seen worse players.'

'I heard you the first time. I was just trying to recall.'

The opposing captain watched the young batsman barely survive an over.

'I'm told cricket is your love,' said the batsman to the captain.

'Quite right,' nodded the older player, 'but don't let that worry you – you just keep on playing.'

The captain refused a request for a player to miss a three-day county match.

'I can't excuse you. If I did I'll have to do the same for every player who wins $100,000 on the Australian Football Pools.'

'My wife's going to leave me if I don't stop playing cricket.'

'Oh dear! That's too bad.'

'Yes, I'll miss her.'

Cricketer: 'How do I stand for a test trial?'
Selector: 'You don't stand, you grovel.'

The visitor was having lunch at Lords with a Member. 'Do we say grace?' he asked.

The Member looked appalled. 'Gad sir, this is Lords,' he thundered. 'We always say "Compton".'

'Why do you call it a hat trick?'
'Because it's performed by a bowler.'

'I can't understand it,' said the captain. 'It was such an important match that I bribed the umpire and yet we lost.'

'Terrible, isn't it,' the wicket-keeper said. 'It's getting so that you can't trust anyone.'

Captain (to dismissed batsman): 'I see you were using old polo today.'

Batsman: 'Why do you call my bat polo? Because it has a sweet sound?'

Captain: 'No, because it seems to have a hole in the middle.'

A hooded streaker ran through the ladies changing-room at the local cricket club while four ladies were undressing.

Three of the ladies remarked that he wasn't her husband, and the fourth stated that he wasn't even a member of the club.

He had dropped five catches during the innings. As he left the field he asked, 'Has anyone got 10p? I want to telephone a friend.' 'Here's 20p,' said the bowler, 'telephone them all!'

The young batsman returned to the pavilion after a short shakey knock.

'That was a lovely stroke,' remarked the incoming batsman.

'Which one?'

'The one when you hit the ball!'

The annual cricket dance was going well and George had coaxed Joan into the changing-room of the pavilion.

Joan: 'Oh no George, you mustn't. Mummy wouldn't like it.'

George: 'Mummy's not going to get it!'

Lady: 'Excuse me son, but I'm making an eiderdown and I would be so grateful if you could supply me with the down.'

Cricketer: 'I'm sorry m'am, I can't help you as I haven't any down. Why ask me?'

Lady: 'Well, your friends told me you had more ducks than anyone else this season.'

In a Test match in Sydney the umpires were taking a lot of verbal abuse from the 'Hill' regarding their decisions on lbw. At the end of an over the two umpires walked to the 'Hill' and seated themselves with the spectators.

'What do you think you're doing, sport?' one was asked.

'Well,' replied the umpire, 'it appears you get a better view from here.'

Sheik: 'It is said he has eighty maidens.'

Cricketer: 'Another five and he can get a new ball.'

The farmer swung at the ball, missed it and it thudded into his box. As he lay doubled up on the ground the friendly wicket-keeper patted him on the shoulder and said, 'Look on the bright side old chap, that's increased the size of your farm – you've got a couple more "acres".'

Mountbatten, Stan Bowls and W. C. Fields.

The gushing bore cornered Denis Lillee at a party.
'Oh Mr. Lillee, I passed by your house today.'
'Thank you very much,' answered the cricketer.

Slowly, the batsman dragged his bat into the pavilion and slumped down on the bench.
'I've never played so badly before.'
'Oh?' said the interested captain. 'You've played before, have you?'

Girlfriend: 'Why is that man running?'
Cricketer: 'He hit the ball.'
Girlfriend: 'Is it not his ball?'

Middlesex and Yorkshire were playing at Lords. A man sporting a large white rose, appeared at the ticket office and asked the price of admission.

'£2, sir,' was the reply.

'Then here's £1. There's only one team worth watching.'

He was a loyal supporter: 'All Nottingham have to do to get the County Championship is to win eleven of their last four matches.'

Man on telephone: '... and after I pour the drinks I'm going to lead you into the bedroom, put you on the bed, strip you naked and make mad passionate love to you – and would you stop telling me the Test match score!'

'Doctor, come quickly. The scorer has swallowed his pen!'
'I'll be there immediately. What have you done?'
'Borrowed another one!'

The bowler was having terrible luck; another coat of varnish and he would have had a wicket. The batsman missed every ball. At the end of the over, the batsman turned to the wicket-keeper and sneered: 'He must be the worst bowler in the country!'
'That would be too much of a coincidence!' replied the wicket-keeper.

'Doctor, I feel like a cricket bat.'
'How's that?'

'Doctor, I feel like a small cricket stump.'
'A little off, eh?'

'Doctor, I feel like a cricket ball.'
'You'll soon be over that.'

'Doctor, I keep seeing ducks before my eyes.'
'Have you seen an optician?'
'No, just ducks.'

'Doctor, every time I lift my bat I feel like crying.'
'Perhaps it's a weeping willow.'

'Doctor, I feel just like an umpire.'

'Don't be silly. There must be someone somewhere who likes you a little.'

They were on their honeymoon and in bed making love. As she stroked his hair her finger touched something in his ear and she said, 'I didn't know you wore a hearing aid.'

'That's not a hearing aid,' he replied, 'that's the earpiece of my radio. I'm listening to "Test Match Special".'

It is rumoured that Cyril Smith is a keen cricketer and bats number seven. Before he lost weight he batted as five, six and seven!

In one match when he was the non-striker, the other batsman asked him to move as he obscured the view.

'Can't see the bowler, eh?' asked Cyril.

'No, the sightscreen,' came the reply.

Captain: 'You're doing all right. He's just in good form. You'll get him with the next ball.'

Bowler: 'Doing all right? He's already hit me for four fours this over!'

The bowler stalked back to his mark banging the ball from hand to hand. A pretty young girl ran up to him and handed him some tablets.

Bowler: 'What are these for?'

Girl: 'Daddy says you're not bowling too well because you're troubled with the wind, so these should help you.'

The bowler had a dreadful match, couldn't find line or length, and his bad spell cost his side the game.

Every night of the following week he practised hard at the nets for the following match on Saturday.

During the match he said to his captain, 'Notice any difference?'

The captain looked at him thoughtfully and replied, 'You've trimmed your moustache.'

The captain called the wicket-keeper to one side and said softly, 'Freddie, you will really have to improve. You missed three catches today.'

'I didn't miss them,' protested the wicket-keeper, 'they just dropped out!'

A cricketer was going through a very lean period. He had been dropped from the first eleven and he had not even been selected for the seconds. His wife had insisted he visit the doctor and on his return home asked the outcome.

'He says I'm suffering from syncopation – whatever that is.'

As his wife didn't know either she consulted the dictionary and read: 'Syncopation – an uneven movement from bar to bar.'

The two old men were talking about their cricketing days.

'What was your highest score?'

'One hundred and eighty-six.'

'Mine was two hundred and ten – not out. And what was your best spell of bowling?'

'Oh no! *You* first this time.'

The cricketer was sitting on the bench suffering the effects of a night out as the captain approached him.

Captain: 'Glad to see you at practice last night.'

Cricketer: 'Oh, was that where I was?'

The day was hot and the batsman wasn't making contact with the ball. After one particularly torrid over, during which he missed every ball, he turned to the umpire.

'What couldn't I do with an ice-cold glass of beer?'

The umpire thought for a moment.

'Hit it with your bat?'

The young batsman had collected three ducks in a row and naturally was rather depressed. The club bore patted him on the shoulder and said, 'Don't worry old boy. Two seasons ago I went through a very bad patch and I'll tell you what brought on the change.'

Overhearing this, the captain enquired: 'What change?'

'You know,' said the club bore, 'it's amazing how my cricketing ability is known. I was at Lords the other day and suddenly there were about twenty people with cameras, all snapping away like mad.'

'Oh, come off it, Ponsonbey.'

'Well, it's true, and if you don't believe me ask Ian Botham – he was standing next to me!'

It was the last John Player League match of 1978 for Gloucestershire, and they were at the bottom of the table.

A customer came to the ticket window. 'May I have two please,' he asked, putting down a five pound note.

'Certainly, sir,' said the cashier. 'Batsmen or bowlers?'

'Who's the batsman dressed like a sailor?'
'Oh, he's the sheet anchor.'

The batsman played forward and pushed the ball slightly wide to mid-off. 'No, no, no!' he yelled to the non-striker who was backing up.

'You know,' said the other batsman as he grounded his bat, 'you sound just like my girlfriend.'

'Jones had a terrible row with his wife last week.'
'What happened?'
'Well, he told her he had to act as night watchman, so she expected a little extra in her housekeeping money.'

The two cricketers were having a drink in their local.

'What do you mean, you had a hard time explaining the cricket match to your wife?'

'She found out I wasn't there!'

A spectator had to be removed from a cricket match as she had kept shouting, 'Kill the umpire, kill the umpire!'

She has since been identified as the umpire's wife.

Tommy studied the examination question thoughtfully. 'What was the main cause of the War of the Roses?'

He wrote in a firm hand, 'The County Championship.'

The match was very dull and not a run was scored for an hour. Suddenly, there was a loud bang as a car backfired. Came a voice from the crowd, 'Tell that man to be quiet, or he'll wake up the scorer!'

The batsman kept playing the ball back to the bowler for over after over. A visitor turned to a home supporter next to him.

'Does that batsman ever score runs?'

'Don't know,' was the reply. 'I've only been coming here for three years.'

The match was very dull and one spectator turned to his friend: 'I'm surprised the spectators don't barrack.'

'Difficult to shout and yawn at the same time,' replied his friend.

'What did Robinson say when he was run out?'
'Shall I leave out the swear words?'
'Yes.'
'He never spoke.'

When Jeff Thompson and Denis Lillee were spear-heading the Australian attack during a tour of England, an English Test batsman was asked when he found these two the least difficult to play. He replied, 'When I'm at the other end!'

A Yorkshire man on a world cruise received the following radio message from his father: 'Regret your grandmother died this morning. We're one hundred and eighty-four for two. Boycott ninety-two not out.'

First Wife: 'What do you think about Joan, she's gone off with the cricket coach.'
Second Wife: 'I didn't know she could drive.'

Husband: 'Only for Archie Brown we would have lost the match today.'
Wife: 'Is he a batsman or bowler?'
Husband: 'Neither. He's the umpire.'

They were short of an umpire so the captain walked into the public bar and asked if there was an umpire present.

One man stepped forward: 'I'm an umpire.'

'Have you stood before?' asked the captain.

'Of course I have, and my three friends here will vouch for that,' was the reply.

'Thank you for offering, but I don't think we'll accept.'

'You don't think I'm an umpire!'

'Quite frankly I don't, because I've never heard of an umpire having three friends.'

The elegant batsman strolled to the wicket and carefully took guard and made his mark with great care. He looked around the field, making note of each fielder, did a spot of gardening, adjusted his gloves then indicated he was ready to receive.

The ball was a yorker and knocked back his off stump. 'Isn't that a shame,' said the wicket-keeper. 'Just as you were getting set.'

The bowlers were getting a lot of stick from the opposing opening pair. The captain decided a new player should have a bowl. He handed the ball to the young man with the advice, 'Keep the ball well up.'

'Don't worry,' was the chirpy reply. 'I know his weakness.'

He bowled four balls and everyone cleared the boundary.

'I see what you mean,' said the captain. 'He's got a weakness for sixes.'

The jilted bride drove to the cricket ground and confronted her fiancé who was buckling on his pads.

'How could you do it? Everyone at the church except you. Why didn't you come?'

'Don't you ever listen,' he answered as he pulled on his gloves. 'I distinctly said only if it rained!'

The annual match between the Royal Ulster Constabulary and the Metropolitan Police was taking place and an Irish policeman had been at the wicket for over an hour and had only scored a single.

Every ball he played the same – a sound defensive shot. Suddenly the umpire raised his finger and said, 'Out'.

'What for?' asked the batsman.

'Loitering with intent,' came the reply.

It was the cricket club's annual dinner and the members settled back for a long boring talk by the president of the club who had the reputation of drivelling on and on. He had been speaking for about five minutes and was still talking of his schoolboy cricketing days, when the captain passed him a note. The speaker glanced at the note, closed his speech quickly and sat down. The members could hardly believe their good luck and asked the captain what he had written on the note.

The captain grinned: 'Only four words: "Your flies are open".'

He was in a reflective mood as he sat staring into the flickering fire. His wife looked at him with a romantic smile. 'Do you remember when you proposed to me?'

'Of course I do. It was behind the pavilion when we were playing Moreton–on–Marsh.'

'You were bold.'

'No I wasn't. I was caught!'

The burly batsman strode out to the wicket and prepared to take the bowling.

'Don't you want guard?' asked the umpire.

'No thanks,' replied the batsman, 'I've played here before.'

When Sir Len Hutton was holidaying in Switzerland, he was out skiing one day when he fell and injured his ankle. He was unable to walk and lay in the snow until a St Bernard dog came along. Sir Len crawled onto its back and the dog set off in a homeward direction.

Night fell and brought heavy snow, and the poor dog lost all sense of direction. When eventually they came to a house both Sir Len and the dog were exhausted. Sir Len hammered on the door and it was opened by a woman.

'What do you want?' she asked.

'We need help. Look, this poor dog is almost dead. He has carried me for miles,' gasped Sir Len.

'Well you can't stay here,' replied the woman. 'This house is for women only.'

'But surely madam, surely,' pleaded Sir Len, 'you wouldn't turn a knight out on a dog like this?'

Yorkshire fast bowler: 'Hi, captain, I've just swallowed the ball.'

England captain: 'Don't worry. The umpire has another one just like it in his pocket.'

Umpire: 'Doctor, I can't sleep at night.'

Doctor: 'How long has this been going on?'

Umpire: 'Oh, about three months.'

Doctor: 'That's terrible. You haven't slept for three months!'

Umpire: 'Oh, I sleep during the matches; it's just at night I can't sleep!'

Cricketer: 'I've been to my doctor and he says I can't play cricket.'

Captain: 'Oh? When did he see you play?'

Cricketer: 'Doctor, every night I have the same dream. I'm opening for England against Australia and I'm always bowled first ball. It's just driving me mad.'

Doctor: 'Well, try dreaming of Farrah Fawcett instead.'

Cricketer: 'What? And miss my turn to bat?'

The batsman kept hooking the ball to the square leg boundary. The captain called to the bowler and said, 'This fellow really has your length, I think I can get him so I'll take the next over.'

When the captain bowled the batsman drove the ball firmly through the covers and it rattled the fence.

'Ah,' said the bowler to the captain, 'I see what you mean. You wanted to make him change direction!'

The captain looked at his middle-aged batting partner who had just had him run out. 'It's a great pity you hadn't taken the game up sooner.'

'You mean I'd be playing Test cricket by this time?'

'No, you'd have already retired!'

The next man in sat on the bench adjusting his gloves, tightening his pads and trying to watch the opening pair struggling against the new ball, doing his utmost not to appear nervous.

Two Saint John Ambulance men arrived and leaving a stretcher on the ground, sat beside the cricketer.

'Then he hasn't been on yet, eh?' asked one man, nudging the player in the ribs.

'Who hasn't been on yet?' asked the player.

'Their new fast bowler of course, who else?'

The Test player stalked into the pavilion and growled, 'That Irish doctor doesn't know what he's talking about.'

'What did he say?'

'He told me I had tennis elbow!'

The fast bowler gazed at his award, the MBE, and growled, 'It's unfair, that's what it is, unfair. Think of it, Sir Don Bradman, Sir Len Hutton, Sir Jack Hobbs and Sir Frank Worrell – all bloody batsman; seems to me the last bowler to be knighted was Sir Francis Drake!'

The batsman mistimed the ball and it just touched his off stump and one bail gently fell to the ground. With great aplomb the batsman replaced the bail and remarked cheerfully, 'Rather a strong wind today.'

'Indeed there is, so be careful it doesn't blow your cap off on your way back to the pavilion,' replied the umpire.

First Starlet: 'It says here Roger scored 22 and was out "Handled ball".'

Second Starlet: 'Oh, how singular!'

The Irish cricketer arrived at the gates of Heaven and was greeted by a cheerful saint. 'Well, well, well! A cricketer from Ireland. You know you're the first one we've got.'

'Well, I hope there'll be many more,' replied the cricketer.

'I'm sure there will be,' smiled the saint. 'You have reached Heaven, but just before you pass through the gates is there any little thing you want to tell me. It can't be much or you wouldn't be here. But perhaps some small incident which is on your conscience?'

'Well,' exclaimed the cricketer, 'there is one thing.'

'What is it, my son?'

'A couple of years ago I was playing for Ireland against the MCC at Lords and the bowler appealed for a catch behind the wicket, but the umpire said

"not out", so although I knew I had touched the ball I stayed on and scored 207 runs.'

'Who won?'

'We did. We beat the MCC by 112 runs, but ever since then I've always thought I should have gone out.'

'Not at all, my son,' boomed the saint, 'you did the right thing. Don't give it another thought. You may enter.'

'I'm very relieved,' replied the cricketer. 'Thank you very much, Saint Peter!'

'Oh, by the way,' grinned the saint, 'I'm not Saint Peter, I'm Saint Patrick.'

'I really had him in two minds that time,' said the bowler, rubbing one side of the ball.

'Indeed you had. He didn't know whether to hit you for a six or four,' replied the captain.

The incoming batsman took guard, did a spot of gardening, tugged at his cap, looked at the scoreboard which showed 2 for 2, scanned the field positions and faced up to the first ball.

It was a fast rising ball which struck him on the left elbow. He dropped his bat and rubbed his injured arm. The second ball was even faster and rapped him on the left hand, he waved it around in agony. He checked his mark and faced his third ball which thudded into his ribs. Slowly he hobbled from the wicket towards the pavilion.

'I say,' shouted the umpire, 'you're not out.'

'No', replied the batsman ruefully, 'but I'm going.'

The president of a cricket club was also the local undertaker, and a dinner was given in his honour on his retirement. In replying to the toast to his health he said he had very happy memories of the club, he appreciated their kindness and although he wished them all long life and happiness if one of the members should die he would bury him free of charge.

There was a loud report at the end of the table and it was found a Scotsman had shot himself.

The club captain was showing the new member around the club and explaining the procedure.

'We have nets four evenings a week. Tuesday, Wednesday, Thursday and Friday.'

'Four evenings? Isn't that a lot? Must one attend all four nets?'

'Oh, not at all, but most of the boys do attend all four as after a net we usually have a little entertainment. For instance, after practice on Tuesday we usually have a poker school.'

'I don't play poker.'

'Oh! Well, after practice on Wednesday night we have a right old booze-up.'

'I don't drink.'

'Well, not to worry. After practice on Thursday night we have a few girls in.'

'I'm not interested in girls.'

'Are you gay?'

'Certainly not!'

'Well, there goes Friday night as well!'

Unknown Commentator: 'The first time you face up to a googly you're going to be in trouble if you've never faced one before.'

First Wife: 'How's your husband today?'

Second Wife: 'His cricket bat is giving him a lot of pain.'

First Wife: 'How can his cricket bat give him pain?'

Second Wife: 'I hit him over the head with it.'

He had a bad day in the field, dropping six catches, and now as he sat huddled in the dressing room he could feel a cold coming on.

'I think I've caught a cold,' he muttered.

'Thank goodness you're able to catch something,' grunted the captain.

The cricket-loving shop steward rubbed his hands with glee. 'Good morning's work, had them all out before lunch.'

The lady was telling of her instruction at the cricket school. 'It's really a wonderful school.'
'But you have been going for six months and you say you still can't bowl. Is the instructor bad?'
'No, handsome!'

The young batsman was apologising to his captain for scoring yet another duck.
'Perhaps I should have another net.'
'Well, make it a fishing one!'

At a charity match Viv Richards was in majestic form and hit the ball all over and, indeed, out of the ground. After a sparkling innings he was caught on the boundary and as he was making his way back to the pavilion he was confronted by an irate spectator.

'You sir, should be more careful,' said the man, 'you only just missed hitting my wife.'

'I'm awfully sorry,' smiled Viv as he walked on.

It was a slow-scoring match and one club member turned to his colleague and said, 'I think the modern game needs more spirit.'

'More spirit?'

'Yes please. I'll have a large brandy.'

'Come on, Thames, you show 'em,' yelled a Yorkshire supporter. 'You're bowlin' well, lad.'

The Kent supporter tapped him gently on the arm. 'Excuse me, but surely you know that Thames is not the name of that fast bowler?'

'Well, that's what we call him back home.'

'Why?'

'Because he's small at the head and big at the mouth.'

Husband (watching TV): 'Joel Garner has come back to bowl with a new ball.'

Wife (knitting): 'Wonderful what doctors can do these days.'

As tradition demanded, the cricket match was played on Christmas Day. The snow covered the ground and the players had difficulty keeping warm. The bowler couldn't get a foothold and the ball kept flying from his hand and 'no-ball' after 'no-ball' was called.

At the end of the over the ice-cold umpire observed, 'It's the cold weather, we're all going to suffer from "no-balls".'

All the players agreed, the match was called off and they all returned to the fire in the clubhouse.

The handsome and dashing batsman had been struck several times in the ribs by the fast bowler and had been taken to the local hospital for a check-up. The pretty nurse told him to go behind the screen and take his clothes off.

Having done so he called, 'I've taken my clothes off, nurse. Where shall I put them?'

'On top of mine,' came the reply.

The batsman was going well against the fast bowlers and was approaching his first ever century, when the twelfth man ran out and whispered to him. The batsman walked over to the fielding captain and said, 'I say Mike, my wife's expecting quins any minute and she wants me at the hospital. Any chance of putting on your slow bowlers?'

'Whatever happened to that hit-and-run driver?'
'He's top of the batting averages in the prison team.'

Ashes to ashes. Dust to dust.
If the batsmen can't score,
The bowlers must.

Then there was the batsman who held up one end all day and got a hernia.

'Now remember,' said the coach. 'You must always get behind the ball.'

'Now, how do I do that?' demanded the Irishman. 'Sure it's the same all the way round?'

'Mummy, why do fairy tales always start with "Once Upon A Time?"'

'They don't always, dear. The ones your father tells usually start, "I never touched the ball ..."'

The annual cricket dance was quite an affair and one of the cricketers who was too drunk to drive, flopped in the back seat of his car and his girlfriend drove.

She hadn't driven far when she was stopped by a policeman and asked to take a breath test. The girl blew into the bag and it immediately changed colour.

'Hello, hello,' said the policeman. 'You've had a stiff one tonight.'

'My goodness,' exclaimed the girl. 'Does that show too?'

When an expectant father telephoned the hospital to see how his wife was getting on, he was connected to the local cricket club instead.

'What's the news?' he asked.

'Great,' came the reply. 'We've got four out already and hope to have the rest out before lunch. And by the way, the last one was a duck.'

Bowler: 'Howzat?'

Umpire: 'How's what?'

Bowler: 'Is he out?'

Umpire: 'No, why should he be?'

Bowler: 'Do you not think the ball would have hit the stumps?'

Umpire: 'I don't know. His leg was in the way.'

The wicket-keeper applied for a trial with a local team. After the trial he was advised that he would not be invited to join the club. However, he asked the captain for a letter of introduction to another club. The captain, not wishing to dampen the young man's enthusiasm, gave him a letter which stated, 'As the wicket-keeper, the bearer is passable.'

He stared gloomily into his drink. His friend nudged him gently.

'I say, you're looking very sad.'

'My wife ran away with my best friend this morning.'

'Oh, that's terrible!'

'Yes, it means we'll have no wicket-keeper this afternoon.'

'That was my best innings ever,' said the eager young batsman.

'Well,' grunted the old pro, 'don't let that discourage you.'

A cricketer died and went to Heaven. One day he looked down to Hell, and there to his amazement saw a cricket ground with fielders out and batsmen at the crease.

'I say,' he said to St Peter, 'look at that. A cricket match about to start. And you call that Hell? Why, I'd love to be playing.'

'So would they,' smiled St Peter, 'but they haven't got a ball!'

It hadn't rained for months and the Indians were worried about the drought. 'Let us do The English Rain Ritual,' said one Indian.

'What is that?'

'When I was in England I saw two men in white coats hammer six sticks into the ground, then two men carrying clubs came out and stood in front of the sticks and then eleven more men came out blowing on their hands. Then one of the white coats shouted "Play", and that's when the rain came pouring down!'

Cricketer: 'Captain I've an idea which may help the team win a few matches.'
Captain: 'Oh good! When are you leaving?'

The cricketer stood at the silver counter in a large store examining a silver dish.
'Solid silver, sir,' pointed out the helpful salesgirl.
'What exactly is it for?' asked the cricketer.
'To keep your nuts in,' answered the girl.
'Thanks all the same,' replied the cricketer, putting down the dish, 'but I think I'll just stick to my leather-covered box.'

Cricketer: 'What's my temperature, nurse?'
Nurse: 'A hundred and one.'
Cricketer: 'That's the first time I've reached a hundred before lunch.'

Bowler (looking at the incoming batsman): 'Is he a good hooker?'

'No, you're thinking of his sister.'

'My wife gave me this lovely ring as a present so I'm praying I don't get hit on it and have it damaged.'

'My wife gave me a new box so I'm praying I don't get hit on it and have it damaged!'

The umpire bent his arm and shouted, 'One short.'

The batsman shook his long golden hair and shrilled, 'Cheeky! How did you know?'

The batsman mistimed the fast bowler and was struck on the pad. The bowler appealed for lbw, but the batsman paid no attention as he stood leaning on his bat, swinging his damaged leg. Slowly the umpire approached him.

'Can you walk?' he asked kindly.

'I think so.'

'Then walk back to the pavilion, son. You're out!'

'I can't bowl a Chinaman but I can bowl an Irishman any time I like,' said the bowler.

'How do you bowl an Irishman?'

'Hand him two glasses of Guinness when he's batting.'

A member of the MCC was asked to state the difference between an Australian Test cricketer and an English Test cricketer.

He straightened his brightly coloured club tie and said, 'An Australian cricketer walks out to bat as if the ground belonged to him, an English cricketer walks out as if he didn't give a damn to whom it belonged.'

'Great pity South Africa was banned from international cricket. Some wonderful players there. Remember the cricketing brothers?'

'Who were they?'

'Pollocks.'

'No need to be rude, I only asked.'

In a tense game a batsman was given out lbw – a decision with which he obviously disagreed. He paced up and down outside the pavilion until the umpire came out.

'I wasn't out, you know,' he said to the umpire.

'Oh no? Look in the paper tomorrow!'

There was a cricketing minister who never waited for an appeal but always walked. One day his captain approached him and suggested he should wait for the umpire's decision.

'I know when I'm out,' replied the minister. 'I'd rather commit adultery than cheat at cricket.'

'Who wouldn't!' retorted the captain.

The batsman played back to the fast bowler. The ball came sharply off the shoulder of the bat and struck him in the face. He fell back on his wicket and sprawled on the ground. As he lay there spitting out blood and broken teeth, the wicket-keeper looked down at him and cheerfully observed, 'Lucky for you it was a no-ball!'

In 1947 when Denis Compton broke the record by scoring eighteen centuries, the story is told that during one match when batting with Bill Edrich for Middlesex he swept a ball from outside the off stump round to fine leg. Completely ignoring the fact that it was Bill Edrich's call, Denis shouted, 'Yes', then, as the fielder swooped on the ball yelled again, 'No!', and as the fielder didn't collect the ball cleanly, finally shouted 'Maybe!'

Doctor: 'What your husband needs is complete rest so he'll be fit for the Test match on Thursday. Here are some sleeping tablets.'
Wife: 'Very good doctor. How many should I give him?'
Doctor: 'Don't give him any, take them yourself.'

Old hand: 'When you're bowling, you must bowl with the head.'
Young hand: 'Is it not hard on the ears?'

The team captain was rather surprised when a horse arrived and asked for a trial. The captain suggested that the horse play in a trial match which was about to begin. 'What number do you bat?' he asked the horse.

'I usually open,' came the reply.

So the horse opened the innings, clad in whites and wearing a brightly coloured cap at a rakish angle over one ear. Every ball he played in the first over was a boundary, four fours and two sixes.

The bowling changed and the batsman pushed the first ball he received gently to the covers and shouted 'One' as he ran. The horse didn't move and the batsman was run out. As he stalked by the horse he growled, 'It was my call. Why didn't you run?'

'Run?' replied the horse. 'Don't be daft, I can't run. If I could run I'd be at Ascot and not playing this bloody stupid game!'

The public school was playing a small village team; the school has won the toss and decided to bat. The first ball shattered the wicket of a rather haughty opening batsman, who, as he walked out remarked to the bowler, 'Lovely ball, my good man.'

'What did you expect?' growled the blacksmith. 'A bloody beetroot?'

Then there was the trainee electrician who failed his examination because when asked what DC stood for, replied, 'Denis Compton'.

The small village ground was crowded, all were there to see the two Australian fast bowlers who were guests on the visiting team.

The village captain won the toss and decided to bat, which was a poor decision on his part. In the first over one fast bowler took all six wickets. The second over produced one run and the fall of the remaining four wickets.

'It must be disappointing for the crowd,' said one of the village players.

'Yes,' agreed the captain, 'but at least they got a run for their money.'

— CLOSE OF PLAY —

The World's Best Motoring Jokes

Edward Phillips

It's generally agreed that the part of the car that causes the most accidents is the nut that holds the wheel . . .

Garage mechanic: 'The trouble is your battery, madam. It's flat.'
Lady driver: 'Oh dear! What shape should it be?'

Traffic policeman: 'Didn't you hear me shout to you to pull over?'
Motorist: 'I'm awfully sorry. I thought you said "Good morning, Chief Constable."'
Traffic policeman: 'That's all right, sir. I just wanted to warn you that the traffic's pretty bad up ahead.'

Whether you're a wheel-nut or a nervous passenger, a motoring maniac or just a back-seat driver, this collection of hilarious anecdotes and one-liners is an essential addition to every glove compartment.

ISBN 0 00 638265 7

The World's Best Skiing Jokes

Ernest Forbes

On the piste or in the bar, planning a skiing trip or tripping off your skis, this look at the lighter side of skiing is essential reading for dedicated snow-addicts and armchair skiers alike.

'My son won a prize in a fishing competition in Gstaad,' said the proud mother.
'Oh, I thought Gstaad was a ski resort,' commented her friend.
'So did I,' agreed the mother, 'but on the postcard he sent me he wrote that he had won a giant salmon.'

'Hello, George,' greeted David as he met his friend. 'Were you on the piste this afternoon?'
'Afraid not. Haven't had a drink since last night,' replied George.

You'll find you're not properly equipped without *The World's Best Skiing Jokes*!

ISBN 0 00 638246 0

The World's Best After-Dinner Jokes

Edward Phillips

Tall tales, naughty narratives and silly spoofs are all part of that hitherto unacknowledged literary genre, the after-dinner joke. Gathered together in this new collection are the *World's Best* specimens of this much-practised but rarely excelled at art form.

The old man was dying and he called his wife and family to his bedside. There were four sons – three fine big boys and a little one. He said to his wife in a weak voice, 'Don't lie to me now – I want to know the truth. The little one – is he really mine?'

'Oh yes, dear,' said his wife. 'He really is, I give you my word of honour.'

The old man smiled and slipped peacefully away. With a sigh of relief, the widow muttered, 'Thank God he didn't ask me about the other three!'

Containing the *crème de la crème* of the joke world, *The World's Best After-Dinner Jokes* is the perfect accompaniment to any meal.

ISBN 0 00 637960 5

☐	WORLD'S BEST AFTER-DINNER JOKES Edward Phillips	0-00-637960-5	£2.99
☐	WORLD'S BEST SKIING JOKES Ernest Forbes	0-00-638246-0	£2.99
☐	WORLD'S BEST MOTORING JOKES Edward Phillips	0-00-638265-7	£2.99
☐	WORLD'S BEST BOSS JOKES Edward Phillips	0-00-638241-X	£2.99
☐	WORLD'S BEST DRINKING JOKES Ernest Forbes	0-00-638242-8	£2.99
☐	WORLD'S BEST DIRTY JOKES Mr J	0-00-637784-X	£2.99

These books are available from your local bookseller or can be ordered direct from the publishers.

To order direct just tick the titles you want and fill in the form below:

Name: _____

Address: _____

_____

Postcode: _____

Send to: HarperCollins Mail Order, Dept 8, HarperCollins*Publishers*, Westerhill Road, Bishopbriggs, Glasgow G64 2QT.

Please enclose a cheque or postal order or your authority to debit your Visa/Access account –

Credit card no: _____

Expiry date: _____

Signature: _____

– to the value of the cover price plus:

UK & BFPO: Add £1.00 for the first and 25p for each additional book ordered.

Overseas orders including Eire, please add £2.95 service charge.

Books will be sent by surface mail but quotes for airmail despatches will be given on request.

24 HOUR TELEPHONE ORDERING SERVICE FOR ACCESS/VISA CARDHOLDERS –
TEL: GLASGOW 041-772 2281 or LONDON 081-307 4052